Warm-Up Test (pages 5–6)

1. lack a dai′ si cal
2. es pouse′
3. in ter mit′ tent
4. pro pin′ qui ty
5. (b)
6. (c)
7. (d)
8. animadversion
9. chicanery
10. [illegible]
11. [illegible]
12. [illegible]
13. epicurean
14. penchant
15. (b)
16. (b)
17. (a)
18. (a)
19. [illegible]
20. [illegible]
21. [illegible]
22. (a)
23. saturated
24. cognizant
25. travesty

Unit 1 (pages 7–8)

1. em′ u late
2. re con′ nais sance
3. es chew′
4. co her′ ent
5. (b)
6. (d)
7. (c)
8. taciturn
9. acquisitive
10. congeal
11. coherent
12. belabor
13. temporize
14. invidious
15. (a)
16. (b)
17. (c)
18. (d)
19. (b)
20. (c)
21. (c)
22. (d)
23. largesse
24. tenable
25. substantiate

Unit 2 (pages 9–10)

1. ce ler′ i ty
2. ac cost′
3. sup′ pli ant
4. his tri on′ ic
5. (b)
6. (d)
7. (c)
8. animadversion
9. talisman
10. halcyon
11. summarily
12. propriety
13. celerity
14. undulate
15. (c)
16. (b)
17. (d)
18. (a)
19. (a)
20. (b)
21. (c)
22. (d)
23. accosted
24. Maelstrom
25. incendiary

Unit 3 (pages 11–12)

1. un won′ ted
2. ver′ dant
3. e vince′
4. pro pin′ qui ty
5. (b)
6. (c)
7. (d)
8. viscous
9. piquant
10. distraught
11. credence
12. utopian
13. propinquity
14. dissemble
15. (c)
16. (c)
17. (a)
18. (b)
19. (d)
20. (a)
21. (b)
22. (c)
23. eulogy
24. exhumed
25. murky

Cumulative Test 1 (pages 13–16)

1. de′ vi ous
2. vis′ cous
3. cred′ ence
4. an i mad ver′ sion
5. em′ u late
6. con geal′
7. pri mor′ di al
8. in tran′ si gent
9. (c)
10. (c)
11. (b)
12. (d)
13. (c)
14. (c)
15. incendiary
16. coherent
17. dissemble
18. verdant
19. undulate
20. largesse
21. unwonted
22. cavort
23. belabor
24. emulate
25. gambit
26. decry
27. taciturn
28. talisman
29. (c)
30. (b)
31. (b)
32. (c)
33. (d)
34. (d)
35. (a)
36. (a)
37. (d)
38. (b)
39. (c)
40. (a)
41. (c)
42. (d)
43. (b)
44. (a)
45. sacrilege
46. substantive
47. germane
48. histrionic
49. verbiage
50. eschew
51.–52. Answers will vary

Unit 4 (pages 17–18)

1. strat′ a gem
2. in car′ ce rate
3. net′ tle
4. pu sil lan′ i mous
5. (a)
6. (d)
7. (b)
8. flotsam
9. ludicrous
10. consummate
11. pusillanimous
12. exigency
13. glean
14. mordant
15. (b)
16. (d)
17. (a)
18. (c)
19. (b)
20. (c)
21. (d)
22. (a)
23. pusillanimous
24. atrophy
25. incumbent

Unit 5 (pages 19–20)

1. id i o syn′ cra sy
2. u biq′ ui tous
3. de praved′
4. fig′ ment
5. (d)
6. (b)
7. (c)
8. ignominy
9. enervate
10. hallow
11. reputed
12. overweening
13. acuity
14. penchant
15. (a)
16. (c)
17. (a)
18. (b)
19. (c)
20. (d)
21. (a)
22. (b)
23. nuances
24. garnered
25. depraved

Unit 6 (pages 21–22)

1. trav′ e sty
2. der′ e lict
3. mo tif′
4. in ter mit′ tent
5. (c)
6. (d)
7. (a)
8. neophyte
9. effigy
10. perspicacity
11. complicity
12. abject
13. travesty
14. agnostic
15. (a)
16. (b)
17. (d)
18. (d)
19. (d)
20. (a)
21. (b)
22. (c)
23. indictments
24. intermittent
25. surveillance

PREFACE

The VOCABULARY WORKSHOP program for Levels A–H includes two student test booklets, Form A and Form B, that accompany each level of the student text. While the format and test sections are the same in both booklets, the items tested in each booklet are completely different, except that they are drawn from the corresponding level of the student text. For example, the Pronunciation section of the test for Level E, Unit 1, begins with *bereft* in Form A and *reiterate* in Form B.

Contents Each test booklet contains the following elements:

- A *Mastery Checklist* of all basic (key) words
- A *Warm-Up Test* introducing the level
- 15 *Unit Tests*
- 4 *Cumulative Tests* for periodic reassessment
- A *Final Cumulative Test* covering all units in the level

Features Each test is made up of groups of exercises focusing on:

- Pronunciation
- Part of Speech
- Spelling
- Definitions
- Synonyms
- Antonyms
- Usage in Context (Sentence Completions)

In addition, the *Cumulative Tests* contain a brief optional exercise, *Framing Sentences*, in which students are asked to provide *original* sentences for some of the taught words.

Use

- The *Warm-Up Test* may serve either as an introduction to the form of the testing program or as a follow-up to the *Diagnostic Test* in the student text.
- Each *Unit Test* may be used as soon as the students have completed work on that unit or at any point thereafter.
- Each *Cumulative Test*, including the *Final Cumulative Test*, is designed for use after the corresponding Review in the student text. These tests may also serve as "lead-ins" to the SAT-oriented Cumulative Reviews in the student text and to the SAT-oriented Prep Worksheets in the corresponding *TEST PREP Blackline Masters*.

The VOCABULARY WORKSHOP series also offers an Online Student Assessment System which allows teachers to quickly and easily create secure, interactive Unit practice and assessment pages that are automatically scored and provide students with immediate, prescriptive feedback. With a Web-based database of nearly 4,000 test items per Level, teachers have the option to individualize tests.

Printed in the United States of America.

ISBN 978-0-8215-8122-3
56789 SCI 16 15 14

TEACHER'S ANSWER KEY
TEST BOOKLETS: FORMS A AND B

Level G

VOCABULARY WORKSHOP

ENRICHED EDITION

JEROME SHOSTAK

Cumulative Test 2 (pages 23–26)

1. my op′ ic
2. con geal′
3. in du′ bi ta ble
4. ig no′ min y
5. per spi cac′ it y
6. fre net′ ic
7. em′ u late
8. fec′ und
9. (b)
10. (a)
11. (c)
12. (c)
13. (a)
14. (d)
15. glean
16. evince
17. indictment
18. enervate
19. disarray
20. encomium
21. garner
22. overweening
23. equity
24. halcyon
25. exhume
26. fiat
27. germane
28. sylvan
29. (a)
30. (d)
31. (c)
32. (d)
33. (b)
34. (b)
35. (a)
36. (a)
37. (a)
38. (a)
39. (c)
40. (b)
41. (b)
42. (c)
43. (d)
44. (d)
45. taciturn
46. penchant
47. incarcerated
48. delineated
49. idiosyncrasies
50. gambit
51.–52. Answers will vary.

Unit 7 (pages 27–28)

1. per ti na′ cious
2. pic a yune′
3. fe lic′ i tous
4. con viv′ i al
5. (c)
6. (d)
7. (b)
8. illusory
9. embellish
10. coterie
11. misanthrope
12. effrontery
13. pertinacious
14. demur
15. (b)
16. (c)
17. (d)
18. (a)
19. (a)
20. (a)
21. (b)
22. (d)
23. jettisoned
24. indigent
25. counterparts

Unit 8 (pages 29–30)

1. sat′ u rate
2. lack a dai′ si cal
3. al lege′
4. re cant′
5. (c)
6. (d)
7. (a)
8. litany
9. juggernaut
10. conciliate
11. arrant
12. slough
13. portend
14. saturnine
15. (d)
16. (b)
17. (a)
18. (c)
19. (a)
20. (a)
21. (d)
22. (b)
23. raze
24. lackadaisical
25. echelon(s)

Unit 9 (pages 31–32)

1. col lu′ sion
2. man′ date
3. red′ o lent
4. ac cla ma′ tion
5. (c)
6. (a)
7. (c)
8. increment
9. vacillate
10. bucolic
11. chary
12. vituperative
13. dilettante
14. shibboleth
15. (b)
16. (a)
17. (d)
18. (c)
19. (a)
20. (c)
21. (d)
22. (d)
23. refulgent
24. acclamation
25. calumniate

Cumulative Test 3 (pages 33–36)

1. de cry′
2. pen′ chant
3. mis′ an thrope
4. im per tur′ ba ble
5. in′ di gent
6. sub stan′ ti ate
7. fat′ u ous
8. par′ ox ysm
9. (c)
10. (d)
11. (d)
12. (b)
13. (b)
14. (a)
15. pedantry
16. inordinate
17. equity
18. irrefutable
19. sophistry
20. exigency
21. fatuous
22. mandate
23. allay
24. perspicacity
25. intransigent
26. maelstrom
27. nettle
28. substantive
29. (a)
30. (b)
31. (d)
32. (c)
33. (d)
34. (d)
35. (a)
36. (c)
37. (a)
38. (c)
39. (a)
40. (d)
41. (b)
42. (b)
43. (c)
44. (d)
45. juggernaut
46. paucity
47. ephemeral
48. derelict
49. consummate
50. acuity
51.–52. Answers will vary.

Unit 10 (pages 37–38)

1. cav′ il
2. pe remp′ to ry
3. re con noit′ er
4. in ure′
5. (d)
6. (c)
7. (d)
8. attenuate
9. penitent
10. shambles
11. oscillate
12. inure
13. peremptory
14. askance
15. (d)
16. (b)
17. (d)
18. (c)
19. (b)
20. (a)
21. (d)
22. (c)
23. foibles
24. decimated
25. fraught

Unit 11 (pages 39–40)

1. mor′ i bund
2. ca bal′
3. a sper′ i ty
4. in ex′ or a ble
5. (b)
6. (a)
7. (b)
8. eclectic
9. flaccid
10. sequester
11. ambient
12. moribund
13. burnish
14. detritus
15. (a)
16. (b)
17. (c)
18. (d)
19. (c)
20. (a)
21. (c)
22. (b)
23. onerous
24. burnishing
25. rudiments

Unit 12 (pages 41–42)

1. gre gar′ i ous
2. de funct′
3. tan′ ta mount
4. om ni pre′ sent
5. (d)
6. (b)
7. (c)
8. mendacious
9. aesthetic
10. fetish
11. interpolate
12. importune
13. tantamount
14. defunct
15. (d)
16. (b)
17. (a)
18. (c)
19. (a)
20. (c)
21. (d)
22. (b)
23. irreparable
24. tantamount
25. languished

Cumulative Test 4 (pages 43–48)

1. a′ tro phy
2. ca vort′
3. de mur′
4. in ter′ po late
5. soph′ i stry
6. jug′ ger naut
7. en co′ mi um
8. un re mit′ ting
9. mael′ strom
10. spo rad′ ic
11. sur veil′ lance
12. im pe cu′ ni ous
13. (d)
14. (b)
15. (d)
16. (c)
17. (b)
18. (a)
19. (b)
20. (a)
21. (a)
22. laconic
23. sumptuous
24. allege
25. collusion
26. burnish
27. complicity
28. fraught
29. murky
30. furtive
31. viscous
32. requite
33. effigy
34. vacillate
35. accost
36. saturnine
37. winnow
38. ignominy
39. counterpart
40. cavil
41. eschew
42. pusillanimous
43. (b)
44. (b)
45. (d)
46. (a)
47. (b)
48. (b)
49. (c)
50. (c)
51. (a)
52. (b)
53. (d)
54. (c)
55. (d)
56. (d)
57. (c)
58. (a)
59. (b)
60. (d)
61. (b)
62. (c)
63. (c)
64. (a)
65. (b)
66. (a)
67. temporize
68. cabal
69. felicitous
70. glean
71. litany
72. benign
73. reputed
74. importuned
75. mandate
76.–80. Answers will vary.

Unit 13 (pages 49–50)

1. mach i na′ tion
2. pu′ ta tive
3. op pro′ bri um
4. ef′ fi ca cy
5. (c)
6. (c)
7. (c)
8. cynosure
9. incongruous
10. deign
11. desiccated
12. canard
13. cognizant
14. mesmerize
15. (b)
16. (c)
17. (c)
18. (a)
19. (d)
20. (b)
21. (a)
22. (c)
23. abstruse
24. ghoulish
25. facade

Unit 14 (pages 51–52)

1. mi nu′ ti ae
2. vi′ sion ar y
3. ca coph′ o nous
4. chi ca′ ne ry
5. (c)
6. (b)
7. (d)
8. moratorium
9. behemoth
10. febrile
11. coup
12. chicanery
13. gainsay
14. blandishment
15. (c)
16. (d)
17. (a)
18. (b)
19. (b)
20. (a)
21. (d)
22. (c)
23. nostrums
24. manifests(ed)
25. wizened

Unit 15 (pages 53–54)

1. a men′ i ty
2. pil′ lo ry
3. sub sist′
4. prom′ ul gate
5. (b)
6. (b)
7. (d)
8. nascent
9. seraphic
10. aperture
11. dissidence
12. iniquity
13. presage
14. progeny
15. (b)
16. (c)
17. (a)
18. (d)
19. (b)
20. (b)
21. (a)
22. (c)
23. dissidence
24. subsist
25. improvident

Final Cumulative Test (pages 55–62)

1. mor a tor′ i um
2. ef fron′ te ry
3. in du′ bi ta ble
4. in vid′ i ous
5. se ques′ ter
6. fat′ u ous
7. im por tune′
8. dis ar ray′
9. sub′ stan tive
10. eu′ phe mism
11. re ful′ gent
12. os′ cil late
13. ir rep′ ar a ble
14. sac′ ri lege
15. men da′ cious
16. e ther′ e al
17. (b)
18. (a)
19. (b)
20. (b)
21. (d)
22. (d)
23. (b)
24. (a)
25. (c)
26. (c)
27. (c)
28. (d)
29. manifest
30. beatific
31. onerous
32. omnipresent
33. misanthrope
34. vituperative
35. rectitude
36. luminous
37. machination
38. abstruse
39. inviolable
40. perfunctory
41. primordial
42. bastion
43. substantiate
44. overt
45. figment
46. jettison
47. travesty
48. lackadaisical
49. hapless
50. calumniate
51. forgo
52. necromancer
53. deign
54. panegyric
55. innate
56. ghoulish
57. (d)
58. (a)
59. (d)
60. (b)
61. (a)
62. (a)
63. (a)
64. (d)
65. (b)
66. (c)
67. (b)
68. (c)
69. (a)
70. (c)
71. (d)
72. (c)
73. (c)
74. (c)
75. (b)
76. (d)
77. (a)
78. (d)
79. (b)
80. (c)
81. (a)
82. (c)
83. (b)
84. (b)
85. (d)
86. (c)
87. (a)
88. (d)
89. amenities
90. gainsay
91. obtuse
92. canard
93. burnish
94. aesthetic
95. peregrinations
96. convivial
97. saturated
98. stratagem
99. moratorium
100. testy

101.–110. Answers will vary.

Warm-Up Test (pages 5–6)

1. man′ i fest
2. foi′ ble
3. com plic′ i ty
4. ir rep′ ar a ble
5. (c)
6. (b)
7. (a)
8. engender
9. deprecate
10. cacophonous
11. countermand
12. imminent
13. charlatan
14. paltry
15. (a)
16. (c)
17. (d)
18. (b)
19. (b)
20. (d)
21. (a)
22. (b)
23. mundane
24. saturnine
25. neophyte

Unit 1 (pages 7–8)

1. ger mane′
2. be la′ bor
3. ac quis′ i tive
4. in tran′ si gent
5. (b)
6. (d)
7. (a)
8. encomium
9. banal
10. coherent
11. eschew
12. intransigent
13. tenable
14. germane
15. (d)
16. (c)
17. (a)
18. (a)
19. (a)
20. (b)
21. (a)
22. (b)
23. emulate
24. reconnaissance
25. taciturn

Unit 2 (pages 9–10)

1. pro pri′ e ty
2. hal′ cy on
3. in cen′ di ar y
4. de′ vi ous
5. (b)
6. (d)
7. (c)
8. sacrilege
9. histrionic
10. pejorative
11. incendiary
12. animadversion
13. brackish
14. gambit
15. (c)
16. (c)
17. (a)
18. (b)
19. (b)
20. (a)
21. (c)
22. (a)
23. undulated
24. halcyon
25. gambit

Unit 3 (pages 11–12)

1. eu′ lo gy
2. ca vort′
3. pri mor′ di al
4. dis sem′ ble
5. (d)
6. (c)
7. (b)
8. verdant
9. propinquity
10. evince
11. eulogy
12. distraught
13. exhume
14. unwonted
15. (b)
16. (a)
17. (c)
18. (d)
19. (c)
20. (d)
21. (d)
22. (a)
23. piquant
24. substantive
25. verbiage

Cumulative Test 1 (pages 13–16)

1. ne far′ i ous
2. my op′ ic
3. mael′ strom
4. in sa′ tia ble
5. pro pin′ qui ty
6. sac′ ri lege
7. con geal′
8. in cen′ di ar y
9. (b)
10. (a)
11. (d)
12. (c)
13. (c)
14. (b)
15. eschew
16. primordial
17. pejorative
18. germane
19. brackish
20. credence
21. halcyon
22. arrogate
23. suppliant
24. distraught
25. dissemble
26. verbiage
27. encomium
28. banal
29. (a)
30. (c)
31. (c)
32. (c)
33. (b)
34. (b)
35. (a)
36. (d)
37. (c)
38. (d)
39. (c)
40. (b)
41. (b)
42. (a)
43. (d)
44. (b)
45. cavorting
46. carping
47. avid
48. temporized
49. maelstrom
50. distraught
51.–52. Answers will vary

Unit 4 (pages 17–18)

1. pe cu′ ni ar y
2. in cum′ bent
3. a′ tro phy
4. flot′ sam
5. (d)
6. (b)
7. (a)
8. glean
9. ludicrous
10. jocular
11. flotsam
12. nettle
13. incumbent
14. bastion
15. (c)
16. (a)
17. (d)
18. (b)
19. (c)
20. (b)
21. (d)
22. (a)
23. recumbent
24. incarcerated
25. flotsam

Unit 5 (pages 19–20)

1. a cu′ i ty
2. gar′ ner
3. soph′ i stry
4. ig′ no min y
5. (b)
6. (a)
7. (c)
8. fecund
9. idiosyncrasy
10. delineate
11. nuance
12. fiat
13. ubiquitous
14. hallow
15. (d)
16. (c)
17. (b)
18. (a)
19. (c)
20. (d)
21. (c)
22. (a)
23. sumptuous
24. nuances
25. acuity

Unit 6 (pages 21–22)

1. der′ e lict
2. in ane′
3. di′ a tribe
4. per spi cac′ it y
5. (c)
6. (c)
7. (b)
8. plenary
9. intermittent
10. travesty
11. sylvan
12. derelict
13. equity
14. testy
15. (d)
16. (b)
17. (b)
18. (c)
19. (c)
20. (a)
21. (b)
22. (d)
23. complicity
24. effigies
25. diatribe

Cumulative Test 2 (pages 23–26)

1. re cum′ bent
2. lud′ i crous
3. feck′ less
4. fi′ at
5. an i mad ver′ sion
6. pen′ chant
7. es o ter′ ic
8. de cry′
9. (d)
10. (c)
11. (c)
12. (d)
13. (b)
14. (b)
15. inane
16. flotsam
17. stratagem
18. ubiquitous
19. mordant
20. exigency
21. travesty
22. moot
23. surveillance
24. sophistry
25. diatribe
26. grouse
27. delineate
28. plenary
29. (a)
30. (b)
31. (d)
32. (d)
33. (a)
34. (d)
35. (b)
36. (c)
37. (a)
38. (d)
39. (c)
40. (a)
41. (d)
42. (a)
43. (d)
44. (d)
45. enervated
46. talismans
47. sacrilege
48. depraved
49. garnering
50. perspicacity
51.–52. Answers will vary.

Unit 7 (pages 27–28)

1. il lu′ so ry
2. fe lic′ i tous
3. mis′ an thrope
4. fur′ tive
5. (b)
6. (c)
7. (b)
8. picayune
9. inordinate
10. pertinacious
11. raiment
12. illusory
13. embellish
14. ephemeral
15. (d)
16. (a)
17. (c)
18. (b)
19. (a)
20. (a)
21. (b)
22. (c)
23. coterie
24. garish
25. embellished

Unit 8 (pages 29–30)

1. coun′ ter mand
2. con cil′ i ate
3. por tend′
4. ech′ e lon
5. (c)
6. (d)
7. (b)
8. saturnine
9. badinage
10. exacerbate
11. recant
12. raze
13. paucity
14. fatuous
15. (c)
16. (b)
17. (d)
18. (a)
19. (b)
20. (a)
21. (b)
22. (c)
23. juggernaut
24. arrant
25. countermand

Unit 9 (pages 31–32)

1. re ful′ gent
2. pal′ try
3. per e gri na′ tion
4. vi tu′ per a tive
5. (d)
6. (b)
7. (c)
8. tyro
9. acclamation
10. pedantry
11. imperturbable
12. increment
13. peregrination
14. redolent
15. (b)
16. (b)
17. (a)
18. (d)
19. (d)
20. (d)
21. (a)
22. (b)
23. redolent
24. paroxysms
25. mandate

Cumulative Test 3 (pages 33–36)

1. con′ cord
2. de mur′
3. tes′ ty
4. in′ cre ment
5. im per tur′ ba ble
6. fat′ u ous
7. e phem′ er al
8. sat′ ur nine
9. (b)
10. (d)
11. (d)
12. (c)
13. (a)
14. (c)
15. overweening
16. paucity
17. raiment
18. juggernaut
19. shibboleth
20. lackadaisical
21. calumniate
22. indubitable
23. redolent
24. juggernaut
25. sumptuous
26. exacerbate
27. indictment
28. paroxysm
29. (b)
30. (b)
31. (a)
32. (d)
33. (c)
34. (a)
35. (a)
36. (d)
37. (d)
38. (b)
39. (c)
40. (a)
41. (b)
42. (a)
43. (c)
44. (c)
45. alleges
46. raiment
47. unremitting
48. reputed
49. glean
50. collusion

51.–52. Answers will vary.

Unit 10 (pages 37–38)

1. lu′ mi nous
2. dec′ i mate
3. re con noit′ er
4. a skance′
5. (d)
6. (a)
7. (b)
8. peremptory
9. fraught
10. inure
11. obtuse
12. cavil
13. attenuate
14. luminous
15. (c)
16. (a)
17. (b)
18. (d)
19. (d)
20. (c)
21. (a)
22. (c)
23. rebuffed
24. charlatans
25. obsequious

Unit 11 (pages 39–40)

1. de trit′ us
2. bur′ nish
3. im pe cu′ ni ous
4. ab′ ro gate
5. (d)
6. (c)
7. (b)
8. rife
9. delectable
10. necromancer
11. sequester
12. flaccid
13. deprecate
14. abrogate
15. (a)
16. (d)
17. (c)
18. (c)
19. (c)
20. (d)
21. (d)
22. (c)
23. cabal
24. impecunious
25. eclectic

Unit 12 (pages 41–42)

1. om ni pre′ sent
2. dis com′ fit
3. in ter′ po late
4. lan′ guish
5. (c)
6. (d)
7. (b)
8. tantamount
9. plaintive
10. impeccable
11. laconic
12. nadir
13. requite
14. aesthetic
15. (d)
16. (c)
17. (b)
18. (a)
19. (a)
20. (b)
21. (c)
22. (d)
23. hapless
24. perfunctory
25. fetish

Cumulative Test 4 (pages 43–48)

1. ir re fu′ ta ble
2. im por tune′
3. os′ cil late
4. flac′ cid
5. dis traught′
6. ob se′ qui ous
7. mor′ i bund
8. se ques′ ter
9. in ter′ po late
10. bu col′ ic
11. be nign′
12. ru′ di ments
13. (d)
14. (c)
15. (b)
16. (b)
17. (c)
18. (a)
19. (d)
20. (a)
21. (b)
22. diatribe
23. detritus
24. perfunctory
25. omnipresent
26. ebullient
27. gregarious
28. dilettante
29. attenuate
30. onerous
31. pedantry
32. abrogate
33. deprecate
34. bestial
35. shambles
36. espouse
37. portend
38. tenable
39. languish
40. laconic
41. cabal
42. aesthetic
43. (c)
44. (d)
45. (c)
46. (c)
47. (c)
48. (b)
49. (a)
50. (b)
51. (b)
52. (d)
53. (a)
54. (c)
55. (a)
56. (c)
57. (b)
58. (b)
59. (a)
60. (d)
61. (d)
62. (b)
63. (c)
64. (c)
65. (a)
66. (a)
67. ignominy
68. charlatan
69. conciliate
70. forgo
71. attenuate
72. eclectic
73. increments
74. plaintive
75. nadir

76.–80. Answers will vary.

Unit 13 (pages 49–50)

1. in con′ gru ous
2. cap′ tious
3. des′ ic ca ted
4. con trite′
5. (d)
6. (a)
7. (c)
8. affront
9. efficacy
10. putative
11. incongruous
12. opprobrium
13. abstruse
14. deign
15. (a)
16. (a)
17. (b)
18. (c)
19. (d)
20. (d)
21. (b)
22. (c)
23. mesmerized
24. engendered
25. machinations

Unit 14 (pages 51–52)

1. eu′ phe mism
2. be a tif′ ic
3. in nate′
4. blan′ dish ment
5. (a)
6. (d)
7. (b)
8. pariah
9. cacophonous
10. visionary
11. manifest
12. gainsay
13. nostrum
14. blandishment
15. (c)
16. (a)
17. (b)
18. (c)
19. (c)
20. (c)
21. (b)
22. (c)
23. behemoth
24. imminent
25. consigned

Unit 15 (pages 53–54)

1. i niq′ ui ty
2. mu′ ta ble
3. ep i cu′ re an
4. res′ tive
5. (d)
6. (b)
7. (c)
8. progeny
9. pittance
10. pillory
11. rectitude
12. panegyric
13. promulgate
14. nascent
15. (b)
16. (b)
17. (a)
18. (d)
19. (d)
20. (c)
21. (b)
22. (a)
23. presage
24. amenities
25. inviolable

Final Cumulative Test (pages 55–62)

1. char′ y
2. bur′ nish
3. in con′ gru ous
4. sum mar′ i ly
5. op pro′ bri um
6. dec′ i mate
7. im pec′ ca ble
8. pit′ tance
9. pan e gy′ ric
10. o bei′ sance
11. an i mad ver′ sion
12. con′ sum mate
13. mes′ me rize
14. a skance′
15. gar′ ish
16. pu′ ta tive
17. (d)
18. (a)
19. (b)
20. (c)
21. (b)
22. (d)
23. (c)
24. (d)
25. (c)
26. (a)
27. (b)
28. (b)
29. macabre
30. arrant
31. mutable
32. nascent
33. cognizant
34. benign
35. indigent
36. euphemism
37. coup
38. captious
39. subsist
40. dissidence
41. deign
42. incarcerate
43. cynosure
44. canard
45. sequester
46. maelstrom
47. abstruse
48. slough
49. discomfit
50. surveillance
51. rectitude
52. consign
53. pariah
54. machination
55. pillory
56. engender
57. (b)
58. (a)
59. (b)
60. (b)
61. (c)
62. (a)
63. (d)
64. (d)
65. (c)
66. (b)
67. (c)
68. (b)
69. (c)
70. (d)
71. (a)
72. (a)
73. (a)
74. (c)
75. (d)
76. (b)
77. (d)
78. (b)
79. (d)
80. (c)
81. (c)
82. (d)
83. (c)
84. (a)
85. (b)
86. (c)
87. (a)
88. (a)
89. sylvan
90. interpolated
91. efficacy
92. mordant
93. wizened
94. rudiments
95. visionary
96. aperture
97. abstruse
98. pertinacious
99. idiosyncrasies
100. tyro

101.–110. Answers will vary.